MW01240848

STAY

in the

FIGHT

Endure to the End

Nicole Williams-Gibbs

Copyright © 2023 by Nicole Williams-Gibbs

Published by Kingdom Writers Publishing 545 Chapel Hill Rd, Springlake, NC

All rights reserved.

No portion of this book may be reproduced in any form without written permission from the publisher or author, except as permitted by U.S. copyright law.

This publication is designed to provide accurate and authoritative information in regard to the subject matter covered. It is sold with the understanding that neither the author nor the publisher is engaged in rendering legal, investment, accounting or other professional services. While the publisher and author have used their best efforts in preparing this book, they make no representations or warranties with respect to the accuracy or completeness of the contents of this book and specifically disclaim any implied warranties of merchantability or fitness for a particular purpose. No warranty may be created or extended by sales representatives or written sales materials. The advice and strategies contained herein may not be suitable for your situation. You should consult with a professional when appropriate. Neither the publisher nor the author shall be liable for any loss of profit or any other commercial damages, including but not limited to special, incidental, consequential, personal, or other damages.

Scripture quotations marked "ESV" are from the ESV Bible® (The Holy Bible, English Standard Version®), copyright © 2001 by Crossway Bibles, a publishing ministry of Good News Publishers. Used by permission. All rights reserved.

Book Cover by Michael Fuller, Jr

First edition 2023

Printed in the United States of America

ISBN: 979-8-9880088-2-8

Table of Contents

Foreword

In a world often fraught with uncertainty, it takes immense courage and resilience. In "Stay in the Fight," we embark on a remarkable journey that explores the depths of the human spirit, revealing the extraordinary stories of those who refused to surrender, who found strength in the face of adversity, and who discovered the true meaning of perseverance.

Within these pages, you will encounter tales of triumph over seemingly insurmountable odds. From the battlefields of war to the internal struggles we all face, this book illuminates the unwavering spirit that resides within every one of us. It reminds us that even in the darkest moments, hope can be found, and the fight can be won.

"Stay in the Fight" is a testament to the indomitable human spirit and the power of resilience. It serves as a beacon for those who have faced or are currently facing their own battles. The stories within these chapters will undoubtedly stir your soul, urging you to persevere through life's most challenging moments.

Through the powerful narratives of individuals who refused to let their circumstances define them, this book offers a roadmap for finding strength, courage, and resilience within ourselves. It teaches us that the fight is not merely about winning or losing; it is about finding the will to keep pushing forward, to stay in the fight no matter what.

As you embark on this transformative journey, allow yourself to be moved, inspired, and uplifted by the incredible stories that await you. Prepare to witness the triumph of the human spirit and be reminded of the limitless potential that resides within each and every one of us.

In the pages of "Stay in the Fight," you will discover that the true victory lies not in the absence of adversity, but in the unwavering determination to face it head-on. May this book serve as a constant reminder that no matter what challenges we encounter, we have the strength to stay in the fight and emerge stronger on the other side. Remember, my friend: when life knocks you down, when the odds seem insurmountable, when giving up feels like the only option, "Stay in the Fight."

Nicole Gibbs and Tonya Hampton

Introduction

On March 16, 2018, I lost my baby and on October 13th the same year, I lost my daddy Apostle LH Williams. Shortly after his death, there was a church split, and I felt like I was going to lose my mind. It felt like my strength was leaving me with each passing moment. I knew that the Word of God declares when we are weak that is when He is strong, but at the time it did not feel like it.

I kept a smile on my face everywhere I went, not wanting to show how vulnerable I was feeling. Matter of fact, I became good at wearing a mask when I was asked, "are you ok?" I would say, "Yes," with my smile, instead of being truthful. No one could tell that I was breaking on the inside, unless they discerned something was wrong. Staying locked inside was the easiest thing for me to do. Isolating myself within myself was so comfortable for me, but at the same time it seemed like the battles were never going to end.

I believed what the word of God said but my heart and my mind were all over the place. I knew pretending, putting on my fig leaves was not what God wanted me to do. Society tells us to fake it until we make it, but I know God does not require me to "fake it." He requires me to "Faith it."

Romans 1:17 says "For therein is the righteousness of God revealed- a righteousness that is by faith from first to last, just as it is written".

To live by faith and not by my emotions or feelings. How I really was feeling was not good and God could not really use me in the state I was in. All day I would hide my pain from the world, and then come home and take out my anger and frustrations out on my family. My husband and children did not deserve to be treated in that capacity. God had truly blessed me with my girls, and the most compassionate, caring, God fearing, voice of reason man of God, that a wife could ever want in Mr. Gibbs. I sure do love me some him.

I would try to seek God with everything in me, whole heartedly, but the warfare was so great. I was unsure which direction to go, who to talk to, and whom to turn to. I knew my only option was the Lord.

Psalms 61:24

From the end of the earth will I cry unto thee, when my heart is overwhelmed lead me to the rock that is higher than I. For thou hast been a shelter for me, and a strong tower from the enemy.

Round 1

The Fight

My heart was in shambles. I would cry myself to sleep some nights because I was dealing with so much, but God's Word does not lie. The Bible says in Ephesians 6:10 "Be strong in the Lord and in the power of his might." I knew I could not be strong in my own strength. He said to me *"My Grace is sufficient for you, my power is made perfect in weakness...* 2 Corinthians 12:9

Through all of it I kept pressing, and I kept fighting. I began to seek the Lord and He took me to 2 Chronicles the 20th chapter and it talked about Jehoshaphat and how a vast army was coming to fight him. I am pretty sure he became fearful like we would today.

 2 Timothy 1:7 states *"The Lord has not given us the spirit of fear but of love, power and a sound mind."* Jehoshaphat pulled himself together and inquired of the Lord. He called a fast, then he began giving instructions.

Obeying the instructions determines if we are going to be victorious or not.

Following instructions

In the Bible, there are many instructions given to believers for the fight against various things such as sin, temptation, and spiritual warfare.

Here are a few key instructions:

Put on the armor of God: In Ephesians 6:10-18, believers are instructed to put on the armor of God to stand against the schemes of the devil. This includes the belt of truth, the breastplate of righteousness, the shoes of the gospel of peace, the shield of faith, the helmet of salvation, and the sword of the Spirit.

Resist the devil: James 4:7 instructs believers to resist the devil and he will flee from them.

Pray: In 1 Thessalonians 5:17, believers are instructed to pray without ceasing. Prayer is a powerful weapon in the fight against spiritual battles.

Put away sin: In Colossians 3:5-10, believers are instructed to put to death their earthly nature and put on the new self in Christ. This means putting away sin and living in accordance with God's will.

Renew your mind: In Romans 12:2, believers are instructed to "not be conformed to this world but be transformed by the renewed mind." This means changing our thought patterns and attitudes to be in alignment with God's will.

Love your enemies: In Matthew 5:44, Jesus instructs his followers to "love your enemies and pray for those who persecute you." This can be a powerful way to overcome spiritual battles and show the love of Christ to others.

Fast and pray: In Matthew 17:21, Jesus tells his disciples that "this kind does not go out except by prayer and fasting." Fasting can be a powerful tool for a spiritual fight and can help believers to focus their hearts and minds on God.

Resist temptation: In James 1:12-14, believers are reminded that they will be blessed if they endure temptation and resist it. This means staying strong in the face of temptation and relying on God's strength to overcome it.

Stand still, and see the salvation of the Lord, which He will accomplish for you today. For the Egyptians whom you see today, you shall see again no more forever. The Lord will fight for you, and you shall hold your peace."

We are not fighting in our own strength but in the strength of the Lord. Jehoshaphat said Chronicles 20:12 *For we have no power to face this vast army that is attacking us. We do not know what to do,* but our eyes are on you. We must know the weapon may form but will not prosper.

The Bible declares that the weapons of our warfare are not carnal but mighty thru God to the pulling down of the strongholds. In the beginning of the book, I stated that the Lord will give instructions and to be victorious, we must follow the instructions the way the Lord gives it. In 2 Chronicles 20:14 the Lord gave instructions as He spoke through the prophet Jahaziel. *"Then the Spirit of the Lord came on Jahaziel son of Zechariah, the son of Benaiah, the son of Jeiel, the son of Mattaniah, a Levite and descendant of Asaph, as he stood in the assembly. This is what Jahaziel said "Listen, King Jehoshaphat and all who live in Judah and Jerusalem! This is what the Lord says to you: 'Do not be afraid or discouraged because of this vast army. For the battle is not yours, but God's. 16 Tomorrow march down against them. They will be climbing up by the Pass of Ziz, and you will find them at the end of the gorge in the Desert of Jeruel. 17 You will not have to fight this battle. Take up your positions; stand firm and see the deliverance the Lord will give you, Judah and Jerusalem. Do not be afraid; do not be discouraged. Go out to face them tomorrow, and the Lord will be with you.'"*

Jehoshaphat bowed down with his face to the ground, and all the people of Judah and Jerusalem fell down in worship before the Lord. Then some Levites from the Kohathites and Korahites stood up and praised the Lord, the God of Israel, with a very loud voice.

Early in the morning they left for the Desert of Tekoa. As they set out, Jehoshaphat stood and said, "Listen to me, Judah and people of Jerusalem! Have faith in the Lord your God and you will be upheld; have faith in his prophets and you will be successful." After consulting the people, Jehoshaphat appointed men to sing to the Lord and to praise him for the splendor of his holiness as they went out at the head of the army, saying:

"Give thanks to the Lord, for his love endures forever." 2Chronicles 20:14-22

Don't be afraid or discouraged. The battle is not yours, it is the Lord's. You will not have to fight in this battle.

Take your position and stand still.

Each instruction serves a significant purpose. When we follow God's instructions, we will get the results. As we can see in Exodus 14:16 Moses received instructions and his instructions were to lift his rod and stretch out his hand over the sea.

The sea divided, and the children of Israel went over on dry ground.

Staying in the fight requires faith. What is faith? Faith is the substance of things hoped for and the evidence not seen. I am quite sure if Jehoshaphat would have gone off his natural eyesight he and his army would have been defeated.

There are times we want to quit, throw in the towel, and give up. There were times I wanted to give up, quit, and throw in the towel. There were times I had said, I do not want to do what I was called to do anymore, because the weight became so heavy. But when we learn to trust in the Lord with all of our heart and
lean not to our own understanding and acknowledge him. God will direct our paths and he will give us a finisher's anointing to finish what he has started in us. The finish line can seem so far away at times, but we must finish the fight, so we do not abort our purpose or our assignments. There are no shortcuts in completing our assignments.

Remember the story of the tortoise and the hare. The hare tried to outsmart the tortoise so that he could win the race, but the tortoise did not detour from the path that he was on he stayed on the path that was set before him. The hare tried to cheat, taking different paths, and even tried to run faster, because the tortoise stayed the course, he was able to make it across the finish line and win. The Bible says what God has started in you he will complete it until the day of redemption. He is doing a great work on the inside of you.

Jehoshaphat stood still and he began to use wisdom with leading his army, *as they began to sing and praise, the Lord set ambushes against the men of Ammon and Moab and Mount Seir who were invading Judah, and they were defeated. The Ammonites and Moabites rose up against the men from Mount Seir to destroy and annihilate them. After they finished slaughtering the men from Seir, they helped to destroy one another.* [2 Chronicles 20:22-23]

My Father taught me how to be strong and not to give up no matter what. I know GOD'S INSTRUCTIONS MAY NOT SOUND LOGICAL, but in following God's instructions not only did he bring me out but I was able to see GOD'S POWER AT WORK. We must know when God gives instructions it is to bless and uplift us. Our obedience to God's instructions does not benefit God, he is already God all powerful, only wise, excellent, and perfect. He is the creator of heaven and earth. Our obedience to God's instruction benefits us. In Scripture we are told **to hear instructions** [Proverbs.1:8;4:1] **to receive it** [Proverbs.8:10] and **hold fast to it** [Proverbs.4:13] The instructions of God tell us what to do and what not to do. With his instructions we do not have to fail or fall apart.

Proverbs 3:5 says trust in the lord and lean not unto thy own understanding in all thy ways acknowledge him and he shall direct your path

Round 2

Don't give up

As a little girl I remember my sister, my two brothers and I helping our daddy with his business. It was called "Williams Painting and Remodeling". He would reconstruct and build houses, churches, barns, ramps, and steps. His hands were anointed, he could look at it and make whatever was needed. Our job was to move debris, bricks, boards, tile, sinks, commodes, siding, you name it. I can remember the fun and exciting times helping our dad and sometimes it would be boring, hot, and long days. One day on our way home we ran out of gas, and the only option was to push the car to the nearest gas station. Which was 12 miles from our house. So, we had to roll up our sleeves and help our dad push the car, so he put the car in neutral and put my sister in the front seat so she could steer the wheel while we pushed. We were so exhausted. We wanted to stop and give up so many times. My dad would ensure us if we kept pushing, we could get anything we wanted when we got to the store. This gave us something to aim for, something to look forward to if we kept pushing. It was hard because we had to go up slight hills and around curves, but we knew we needed to keep going. Daddy kept telling us we were almost there, but the more he said it the farther away the store seemed to be. We cried but then we took our mind off how much longer we had until we arrived at the store. We started singing old songs and praising God. We had a good time. We sang and praised God so much we did not even realize we had arrived at the gas station. Whew, talking about someone excited. We were so happy that we finally arrived at the gas station. It was then I realized that it is in your praise and your worship that you will see victories, Hallelujah.

We should be focused on God and not our problems. Look at Jehoshaphat the Bible says that he led the army with praise and worship, and it caused an ambush which caused the enemies to turn on each other, and Jehoshaphat's army claimed the victory. Not just the victory but the blessing as well. The Bible says that they gathered all of the spoils for three days. Hallelujah!

Another example of not giving up in the fight is in the book of Exodus, when the Egyptian army caught up with the Israelites and all seemed lost. The Israelites complained, "is it because there are no graves out here you brought us here to die." They were trapped between a wall of soldiers and a sea of water. In panic, they cried out to both Moses and God, and both of them responded. Moses said, "Stand still, and see the salvation of the Lord." [Exodus 14:13]. And God told them, "Go forward"

[Exodus 14:15]. While that may seem to be contradictory advice, both commands were from God, they did not give up.

Persevere in prayer: In Luke 18:1, Jesus tells his disciples a parable to show that they "should always pray and not give up." Prayer is a powerful weapon in any fight or spiritual battle, and believers are encouraged to persevere in prayer even when they do not see immediate results.

Endure suffering: In Hebrews 12:1-3, believers are encouraged to "run with perseverance the race marked out for us" and to "fix our eyes on Jesus, the author and perfecter of our faith." This includes enduring suffering and persevering through difficult circumstances.

Stand firm in faith: In 1 Corinthians 15:58, believers are instructed to "be steadfast, immovable, always abounding in the work of the Lord, knowing that in the Lord your labor is not in vain." Standing firm in faith requires perseverance and endurance in the face of opposition and difficulty.

Press on toward the goal: In Philippians 3:12-14, the Apostle Paul writes that he presses on toward the goal of knowing Christ and attaining the resurrection from the dead. This requires perseverance and determination to keep moving forward, even when faced with obstacles.

Be of good courage: In Joshua 1:9, God commands Joshua to be strong and courageous and to not be afraid or discouraged, for God is with him wherever he goes. Courage and perseverance are important in the fight against any fight or attack as believers must overcome fear and doubt to press on in faith.

These examples, along with many others found in the Bible, show the importance of perseverance and not giving up in the fight against any battle. By relying on God's strength and guidance, believers can overcome obstacles and press on toward the goal of knowing and serving Christ. First, the Israelites had to "stand still" long enough to get instructions from God. What if they had rushed into the Red Sea without consulting the Lord? It could have turned out differently or it could have been catastrophic.

But in standing still, they heard God's instructions, which included both what they were to do—move on, and what Moses was to do—stretch out his hand over the sea in obedience and God would part the waters.

Do circumstances have you stuck, we must take time to consult God and His Word. Then, use His instructions, move ahead and let God guide you, let GOD FIGHT FOR YOU and YOU WILL COME OUT VICTORIOUS EVERY TIME!

Round 3

Don't be Discouraged

Discouraged means having lost confidence or enthusiasm; disheartened.

When you make up in your mind that you are going to stay in the fight, there are times you will get discouraged. For example, there were countless times I felt discouraged and felt like I could not go on. Felt I had depleted all the fight in me, but I was reminded through the word of God, David found consultation through the word of God, and had to encourage himself in the Lord. [1 Samuel 30:6-8.]

Encouraging oneself can be challenging. It was challenging for me because I wanted someone else to do it. I wanted someone else to pray for me, I wanted someone else to speak into my life, I wanted someone else to see what I was going through. God did not send anyone else, he gave me the command, he told me what to do through his word. As I began to speak his word and give myself pep talks, I knew I had what it took to stay in the fight. The enemy wanted me to take the easy way out, by just simply giving up, then God reminded me of the story of Hannah and Peninnah.

Hannah wanted to have a child but could not. However, Peninnah could have children and would pick on Hannah and tease her because she was not able to have children. I'm pretty sure Hannah felt defeated, but Hannah did not give up even though she was discouraged at times. She kept pressing, she fasted and prayed, she stayed in the fight. By desperately wanting to have children she stood on the word of God, she held on to faith. Hannah also made a vow to the Lord. She began to say to God, if you allow me to have a child, I will give him back to you. God brought her out because Hannah did the work.

I did not want to do the work required of me to stay in the fight. I am good at walking away when things are not working out for me. I just wanted the chips to fall where they may. However, just like the Lord remembered Hannah, he reminded me he had not forgotten me, and he was fighting for me. I heard in my spirit a loud echo "I am fighting for you daughter. Don't be dismayed you got this, continue to be strong in me." Those words he spoke to me pushed me back in the ring. I felt like Sophia in the movie, The Color Purple, when she said, "all my life I had to fight, nothing ever came easy for me."

God never left my side. Fighting takes stamina. There were things that knocked me down and literally knocked the wind out of me. I remained encouraged, I kept my mind on Him and He kept me in perfect peace. I did not lose my focus. Sometimes I had to get away by myself, go on nature walks, take myself out to eat, just to get encouragement and I would come back so refreshed, so revived to stay in the fight a little longer.

Round 4

Take your Position

The Bible says that 2 chronicles 20: 5-9 *Then Jehoshaphat took position before the assembled people of Judah and Jerusalem at The Temple of God in front of the new courtyard and said, "O God, God of our ancestors, are you not God in heaven above and ruler of all kingdoms below? You hold all power and might in your fist—no one stands a chance against you! And didn't you make the natives of this land leave as you brought your people Israel in, turning it over permanently to your people Israel, the descendants of Abraham your friend? They have lived here and built a holy house of worship to honor you, saying, 'When the worst happens—whether war or flood or disease or famine—and we take our place before this Temple [we know you are personally present in this place!] and pray out our pain and trouble, we know that you will listen and give victory.'* In other words Jehoshaphat prayed. Then Jehoshaphat expressed his confidence in the Lord to handle the problem.

I can recall just this year I wanted to take matters into my own hands because my mind kept replaying over and over all the things that I went through. My health was attacked. I was rushed to the hospital because I was experiencing unbearable pain. I was immediately taken in for testing. I had CAT scan and an MRI. The doctor informed my husband that they were going to have to admit me to the hospital and do emergency surgery. The doctor also told him that I got there just in time, or it could have been another way. Hallelujah! He told my husband that my bowels had obstructed, and I needed a hernia repair. I thank God I got there when I did. I heard everything the doctors were saying, and in my mind, I was rebuking the enemy, but fear also tried to grip my heart. But the Lord reminded me I shall live and not die and declare the word of the Lord. So, I went through the surgery and came out fine. Then a day or so went by and I started having major complications. I could not hold anything down or put anything out. The nurse had to put a GI tube down my nose into my stomach [worst feeling ever]. By this time fear gripped my heart again, the fear was so strong that I had an extremely hard time sleeping at night. I remember lying in that hospital bed. I knew that God wanted me to trust him, so I started listening to praise and worship night and day, while I was in the hospital. Reading the word of God, but most of all praying like Jehoshaphat did. He positioned himself for the win, and so did I.

Surrender to God: In order to position oneself in the fight according to the word of God a person must first surrender their lives to God. This involves acknowledging their need for a savior and putting their faith in Jesus Christ as Lord and Savior.

Put on the armor of God: In Ephesians 6:10-18, believers are instructed to put on the full armor of God to stand against the schemes of the devil. This includes the belt of truth, the breastplate of righteousness, the shoes of the gospel of peace, the shield of faith, the helmet of salvation, and the sword of the Spirit, which is the word of God.

Seek God's will: In order to position oneself in the fight according to the Bible, a person must seek God's will and purpose for their lives. This involves spending time in prayer and studying the Bible to discern God's plan.

Walk in obedience: Once a person has discerned God's will, they must walk in obedience to his commands. This involves living a life of holiness and righteousness, and making choices that are in alignment with God's will.

Trust in God's strength: In the fight against spiritual attacks a person must rely on God's strength and power. This involves trusting in God's promises and having faith that he will provide the strength and resources needed to overcome obstacles and challenges.

When a person positions themselves in the fight according to the Bible, they become empowered to overcome spiritual battles and to live a life that is pleasing to God. By surrendering to God, putting on the armor of God, seeking his will, walking in obedience, and trusting in his strength, believers can experience victory and spiritual growth in their lives. The Lord reminded me again that the battle is not mine but belongs to him. He is the author and finisher of my faith.

Round 6

Pressing through Loss

I remember having a weird craving for olives and blue cheese one day and a nauseous feeling the next day. I was like, wait a minute what is really going on? I thought maybe I could be pregnant. So, I took a pregnancy test, and it came back positive. This was an exciting time for my husband and me. We looked forward to going to the doctors' appointments together, talking about pregnancy, belly rubs and eating different foods, LOL. As soon as I found out I was pregnant I called my doctor to make an appointment. My first appointment was so far away, almost a month. When the time came for my appointment, we were overjoyed and could not wait. The doctor checked everything out and all was well with me and the baby. We were doing superbly. They checked all my blood levels and all was well, because of my age I was considered a high risk pregnancy. So, the doctor sent me on my way. By the next appointment I was at least eight weeks and still excited and enthusiastic that we were finally pregnant with our third child! Yay! Time went by, then we were due back for the, and the ultrasound and the doctor asked me a series of questions: Have you felt pregnant? When was the last time you felt movement? Have you felt any movement lately? I began to answer all the doctor's questions while they did several tests to ensure the baby was ok; however, it was not good. As a matter fact I got news that I did not want to hear, "your HGC levels are not where they are supposed to be." I began to inquire about what that meant, and the doctor began to tell me that your HGC levels must be above 5000 because I was between 13-16 weeks [about 3 and a half months]. Mine was below 5000 and I was at risk for a miscarriage at any given time. While she was talking and giving me the news, my mind shifted somewhere else because that was not the news I wanted to hear. I did not receive anything the doctor was telling me. It was like it was going in one ear and out the other. In the back of my mind, I kept speaking the word and I kept saying to myself whose report shall you believe? I shall believe the report of the Lord. I kept the faith. After getting the news I left the office still believing that my baby was going to make it.

By this time, I called my husband to give him the news and went back to work. I felt fine and I kept saying I am not going to have a miscarriage. I got back to work and worked for an hour. Then I started cramping, and I tried to work through it. However, the pain was becoming intense. By this time, I am asking if I could go home. I grabbed my things and started my car, but I could not make it. By the time I got to the door a gush of fluids came out of me and I ended up on the floor. Blood was everywhere. Because I worked at a hospital, they called the rapid response team and rushed me to the ER. There I was having a miscarriage, the thing that I believed was going to turn around for us. I was a nervous wreck because I never experienced anything like it before. Tears were rolling down my face because I knew I had just lost my baby, the one thing we were excited about weeks prior. At this moment I felt like a failure, I felt helpless. We lost the one thing that we prayed and believed God for. By this time, I called my husband to let him know that we lost the baby and his whole world shattered into pieces. He took it very hard; he did not want to discuss it for a long time. It was not easy for us; months went by, and my husband still could not talk about it. We became angry, confused, and even vexed. We could not understand why God would bless us and then take it away. It was another blow below the belt, so I thought.

 I finally got to the place where I could talk about what had happened. However, a couple of months went by, and I ended up in the hospital again. This time I was having the worst pain in my back and stomach. I was told that I had an infection in my body, and I was going to need to have surgery again. It didn't look good for me. The Lord let me know during my stay in the hospital that losing my baby was part of the process, if I would have carried full term it would have terminated my life. He knew what was taking place in my body even when I didn't. All the glory belongs to God. I stayed in the fight. Yes, it was painful to deal with, but I held on to God's unchanging hands and His word says that He would never leave me nor forsake me and that He was fighting for me.

During this time of trying to regroup, my husband and I went to the beach to get away. We just sat by the waves to clear our minds. God said He will keep us in perfect harmony if we keep our minds on Him. We prayed and praised as much as we could, to keep the enemy from coming into our thoughts and mind, but it was not easy. It is always easy to praise and worship God after He brings you out but what about before the battle is actually won.

We had to trust in God's sovereignty: In Psalm 139:16, the Psalmist writes that God knows the days of our lives before they even come to be. Believers can find comfort in knowing that God is in control and that He has a plan for our lives, even when we do not understand it.

Lean on the comfort of the Holy Spirit: In John 14:16, Jesus promises to send the Holy Spirit as a comforter and helper to believers. Those who are grieving the loss of a child can find comfort in the presence of the Holy Spirit and in the knowledge that God is with them in their pain.

Galatians 6:2, say to bear one another's burdens and to support one another in times of need. Those who have lost a child in a fight can find strength and support from their community of faith, as well as from family and friends.

Look forward to eternal life: In 2 Corinthians 5:1, Paul writes that believers have a building from God, an eternal house in heaven. Those who have lost a child in a fight can find hope in the knowledge that their child is with God and that they will one day be reunited with them in heaven.

Proverbs 3:5-6, says to trust in the Lord with all their hearts and to lean not on their own understanding. Those who are grieving the loss of a child can seek God's guidance and direction for their lives as they move forward.

While there are no easy answers or quick solutions for those who have lost a child in a fight, the Bible offers comfort, hope, and guidance for those who are grieving. Believers can trust in God's sovereignty, find comfort in the presence of the Holy Spirit. It was during these trying times being faithful to God strengthened me and encouraged me. As I continue to reflect on the goodness of the Lord it serves as a reminder of God's steadfast presence in my life. The battles I faced felt impossible and seemed without any solution, but I knew God was the only resolution.

In this battle the Lord gave me new weaponry. I knew that I had to use my weapons. I had to bear down and fight. The devil knows where your vulnerability is and he tries to get you at that point, but I did not let him see me sweat. I needed skills in the fight, and I also had to activate my faith. With persistence and consistency, I became relentless, limitless, but most of all unstoppable. Staying in the fight elevated me and catapulted me to a place of victory.

 The only way to stay in the fight was to humble myself and listen to the Holy Spirit. I had the opportunity to listen to those who have been through some things, those who have had tough blows, those who had those hard hits, hard falls and were able to get back up even when they thought they could not. They were able to shed light and wisdom for me. I was able to be strengthened by their stories, their moments, and nuggets, and use them in my experiences and the things I was facing.

Phil 3:13-14 says Brethren, I count not myself to have apprehended: but this one thing I do, forgetting those things which are behind, and reaching forth unto those things which are before, I press toward the mark for the prize of the high calling of God in Christ Jesus.

Round 6

Absence of My Dad

My dad was my world, he taught me everything I know, he was fun, loving, family oriented, and a pastor. I loved my father so much there was nothing that I would not do for him. I was daddy's girl at heart. He was very smart, talented and was gifted with his hands. However, while growing up my dad along with my mom kept us in church and at an early age, I grew to know the Lord. During the years my parents became pastors, and he would use my sister and I in his ministry. I was the praise and worship leader, and my sister was the praise dancer. Working in ministry with my father was what I loved. I loved being by his side, being able to assist in any capacity that I could to the Glory of God. I prayed and covered my father as he traveled in over 22 states preaching the gospel. I was his driver and one of his armor bearers as well.

My father mentored and trained me in ministry. He imparted so much into me. He believed I could do it even when I did not believe I could do it myself. I counted it as a privilege and honor for him to use me in his ministry. My father was hard on me at times, because he knew what was on the inside of me. I just wanted to be a typical teenager, but no matter what, even at a young age he would push me in the ministry. Do not get me wrong, he never stopped me from going after my goals and dreams. He would always encourage me to be all I could be. It was so exciting at times to work closely with my dad, cultivating the gifts that were deposited on the inside of me walking along him was always teachable moments and experiences. Very seldom did he treat me like a daughter he always treated me like a leader that God was molding. After I sang, he would encourage me and after I preach, he would critique me and tell me what I did wrong. He would always give me the bad and the good. These teachings were humbling, and I was honored to get these moments. Years went by and he began to reveal to me what my ultimate calling was, which the Lord revealed to me when I was a freshman in college at the age of 18. He began to say you know you are going to pastor this ministry right; I did not respond I just looked at him and smiled. I let it go over my head, and he would say it frequently more than I wanted to hear, but he was so serious. He would announce it before the congregation so they would be aware. One thing about my dad, Apostle Williams, he did not play when it came to ministry and God's people. During the years my father was pastoring his health started declining and he had a massive heart attack, but he didn't let that stop him. He survived and continued in ministry. My father was the strongest man I knew. It did not matter what he was faced with, he never let anything keep him down, he was a true leader and servant at heart. He exemplified what it was to stand in the strength of God. I admired his strength. It did not matter what was going on with him, he always showed up for his family, his friends, his enemies, his church family, most of all doing God's will. This man of God never complained, he kept right on doing God's will.

However, a couple of years went by, and my father got sick again, this time he had a massive stroke. My heart dropped when I got the call that my daddy had a stroke and had to be rushed to the hospital. I got to the hospital and gathered everyone, and we began to pray for divine reversal in his life. He was not doing well so they had to rush him to Carolinas Medical Center in Charlotte where they were able to get him stable. All kinds of things started running through my head. Lord, is my father going to die, what am going to do if something happens? Not just my father but my pastor Apostle L.H. Williams. Days went by and he was doing fairly well; he knew who everyone was. His speech was a little off, delayed on his left side a little, and he had to learn how to walk and write over again. God is good, it could have been worse... but God. It was time for my dad to be released from the hospital, and he had to have help with everything, but hey! I was grateful he was still alive. During his recovery he would still teach and preach the word of God.

The time came near for my ordination service to be ordained as Pastor of Life Changing Ministry alongside my husband. Before the ordination service he called us to the table and gave us specific instructions he set things in order. Ordination day came September 30, 2018, and we were placed in position. 21 days later my father died. I was so broken, confused, vexed, perplexed, and had questions for days I could not understand. My heart was heavy. I was dealing with all these things when my father passed away. I wanted him to see the fruits of his labor, sit back and enjoy this next phase in ministry, and be proud of me. I wanted him to see the impact he made in my life. This was not an easy one to fight through. I almost had no more fights in me. I almost lost my zeal, my passion and drive for ministry, I did not want to preach, sing, nor did I want to pastor anymore. My dad was my world. I walked alongside him for over 27 years. When my dad died it felt like a piece of me died too. I could not stop the tears from flowing for a long time. I was burdened and I was grieved for a long time after his death. I know at least for 2 years.

However, I was riding out of town with my husband for vacation, and I received a phone call from my mentor Apostle Karen McNair, and she said Pastor

Nicole I need you to preach for me, and I try to produce every excuse as to why I could not. She didn't make me but she began to declare the word of God in my life. I am sure the Apostle did not know what was going on inside of me, but the Spirit of the Lord did, The Lord knew what I needed to come out of the cave, out of hiding. So, I accepted the invitation, but I was still feeling heavy, weary, and in my feelings. I trusted God and continued to fight. Plus, I knew if my father were still here on earth he would not want me to be in this state of mind no matter what. The loss of my father was another blow, a hard hit. That knocked the wind out of me.

God really does give his toughest battles to his strongest warriors. I never knew how strong I was until I went through these different battles. However, it was all a part of the process, I learned that the process does not feel good but it is good for you.

Process is a series of things that happen which are carried out to achieve a particular result.

He was processing me for purpose and destiny for my life. Oftentimes I would sit and wonder where I would be if I had not endured every battle in my life, what would be the outcome of my purpose. He let me know he took me through these series of battles, to increase my faith, to refine my character, to mold and shape me to be able to stay in the fight. When God has something for you to do the enemy tries to block your path, but God will show you how to navigate through the fight. Sometimes you may need assistance to get back up. Stay in the fight! I fought when people walked out on me. Stay in the fight! I fought when I did not have anyone to turn to. Stay in the fight!

I fought to love, I fought to continue, I fought to live, I fought to get out of bed, and I fought within myself, my doubts, my weaknesses, weariness, my fears, lies, haters, gossipers, and betrayers. Stay in the fight! I felt I could not go on because I was fighting with myself.

In conclusion, the Bible encourages believers to stay in the fight, to persevere and to trust in God's strength and guidance. When we position ourselves in the fight according to the Bible, we can experience victory over sin and spiritual battles, grow in our faith and deepen our relationship with God. Find peace and hope that come from trusting in God's plan and purpose, while experiencing the joy that comes from serving God. Even in the face of loss and difficulty, the Bible provides comfort, hope, and guidance for those who are grieving, reminding us to trust in God's sovereignty, lean on the comfort of the Holy Spirit, find strength in community, look forward to eternal life, and seek

God's guidance for the future. By staying in the fight and relying on God's strength and guidance, believers can experience the fullness of life that God has planned for them.

Round 7

Knock Out

Additionally, the Bible teaches that staying in the fight requires spiritual discipline, such as prayer, reading and studying the Bible, and having faith. In Ephesians 6:10-18, Paul describes the armor of God, which includes the belt of truth, the breastplate of righteousness, the shoes of the gospel of peace, the shield of faith, the helmet of salvation, and the sword of the Spirit, which is the word of God. These pieces of armor represent various aspects of our spiritual lives and are meant to protect and equip us for the fight.

Furthermore, the Bible emphasizes the importance of perseverance even in the face of trials and hardships. In James 1:2-4, James encourages believers to count it all joy when they face trials, because trials produce perseverance, and perseverance produces maturity and completeness. By staying in the fight, believers can develop spiritual maturity and a deepened faith that can withstand even the toughest challenges. Ultimately, staying in the fight according to the Bible requires a deep trust in God's plan and purpose, even when it is difficult to understand or when we face setbacks and failures. As believers, we can trust that God is with us in the fight, that

He is working all things for our good, and that He will bring about His plans and purposes in His own time and in His own way.

Another key aspect of staying in the fight according to the Bible is to remember our identity in Christ. As believers, we are the children of God, forgiven and redeemed by His grace through faith in Jesus Christ. In Christ, we have victory over sin and death, and we are given new identities as co-heirs with Christ. When we face trials and struggles, it is important to remember our identity in Christ and to draw on the strength that comes from knowing Him.

Also, the Bible teaches that staying in the fight requires humility and a willingness to learn and grow. In Philippians 2:3-4, Paul writes that we should do nothing out of selfish ambition or vain conceit, but in humility we should consider others better than ourselves. By remaining humble and teachable, we can learn from our mistakes and failures, and grow in our faith and relationship with God. The Bible emphasizes the importance of staying focused on our mission and purpose as believers. In Matthew 28:19-20, Jesus gives the Great Commission, instructing His disciples to go and make disciples of all nations, baptizing them in the name of the Father, and of the Son, and of the Holy Spirit, and teaching them to obey everything He commanded them. As believers, our mission is to share the love and message of Jesus Christ with others, and to be His hands and feet in the world. By staying focused on our mission and purpose, we can find strength and motivation to continue in the fight, even when it is difficult or discouraging.

Staying in the fight according to the Bible involves spiritual discipline, perseverance, trust in God's plan and purpose, a deep understanding of our identity in Christ, humility and a willingness to learn, and a focus on our mission and purpose as believers. By following these principles, we can grow in our faith, experience victory over spiritual battles, and fulfill our calling as children of God.

He told me I could take my gloves off now because the battle had been WON!

Stay in the Fight!

Made in the USA
Middletown, DE
29 October 2023

41517474R00027